Seychelles:
A Guide to the Best Beaches, Activities, and Cultural Experiences

Table of Contents

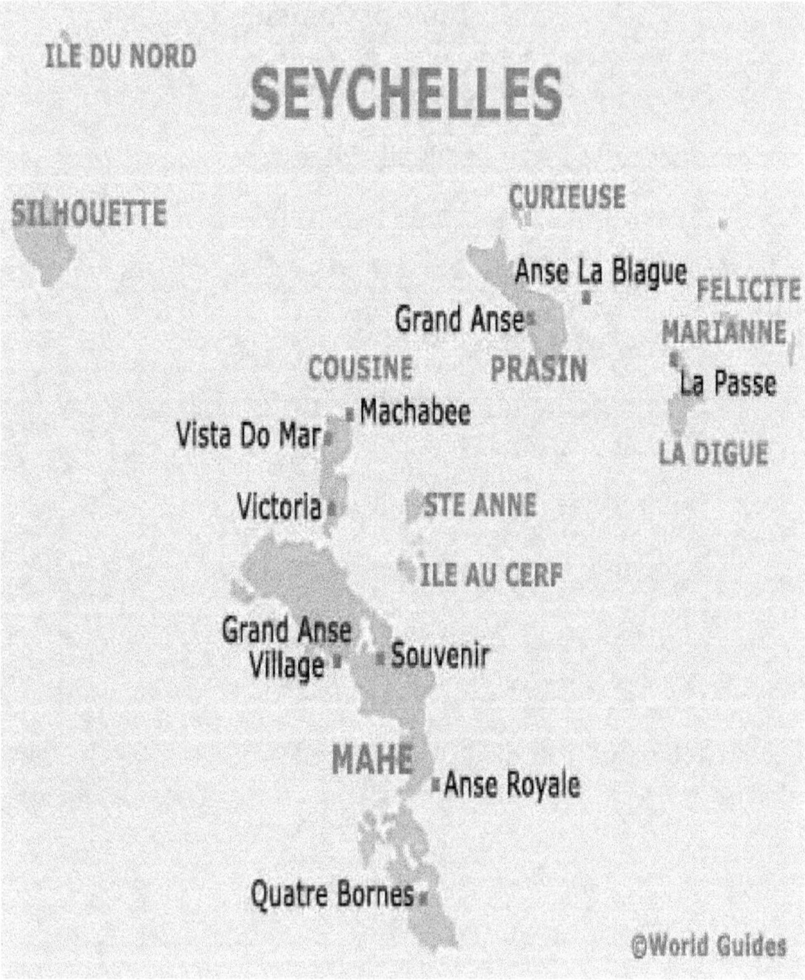

ÎLE DU NORD
SEYCHELLES
SILHOUETTE
CURIEUSE
Anse La Blague
FELICITE
Grand Anse
MARIANNE
COUSINE
PRASIN
La Passe
Machabee
Vista Do Mar
LA DIGUE
Victoria
STE ANNE
ILE AU CERF
Grand Anse
Village
Souvenir
MAHE
Anse Royale
Quatre Bornes
©World Guides

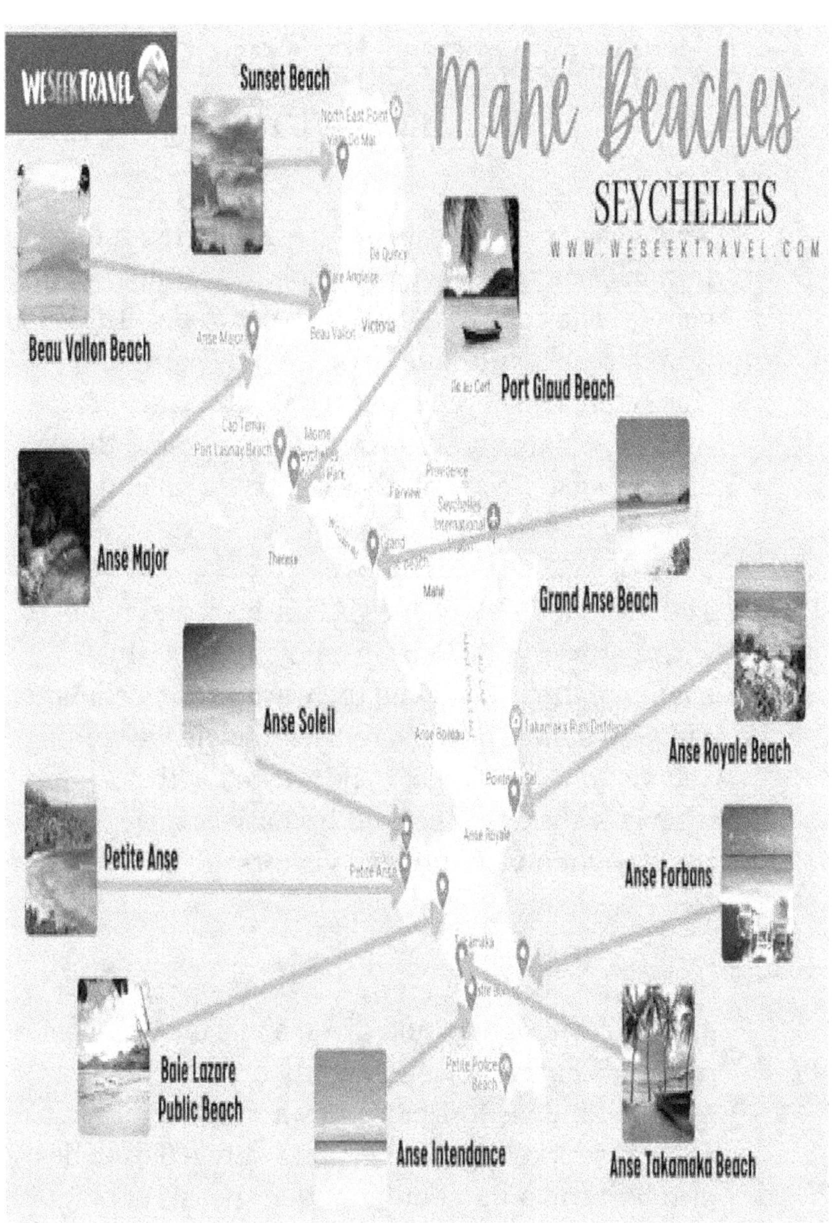
WESEEK TRAVEL
Mahé Beaches
SEYCHELLES
WWW.WESEEKTRAVEL.COM
Sunset Beach
Beau Vallon Beach
Anse Major
Anse Soleil
Petite Anse
Baie Lazare Public Beach
Anse Intendance
Port Glaud Beach
Grand Anse Beach
Anse Royale Beach
Anse Forbans
Anse Takamaka Beach

Introduction to Seychelles lifestyle

Seychelles is a tropical paradise located in the Indian Ocean, with a population of around 96,000 people. The country is made up of 115 beautiful islands, each with their own unique charm and character. The Seychellois people are a mix of African, Asian, and European cultures, and this diversity is reflected in the country's rich and vibrant culture.

The lifestyle in Seychelles is laid-back and relaxed, with a strong emphasis on enjoying the natural beauty of the islands and the warm, sunny climate. The Seychellois people are friendly and welcoming, and visitors can expect to be greeted with a smile wherever they go. The country has a strong tradition of hospitality and visitors are always made to feel welcome.

Seychelles is known for its stunning beaches, crystal-clear waters, and diverse marine life. The country's natural beauty is a major attraction for tourists, and visitors can enjoy a range of activities such as snorkeling, diving, and fishing. Seychelles is also home to a number of unique species of plants and animals, and visitors can take guided tours of the country's national parks and nature reserves to learn more about the country's rich biodiversity.

Overall, Seychelles is a unique and fascinating destination with a lot to offer visitors. From its stunning natural beauty to its rich and diverse culture, Seychelles is sure to leave a lasting impression on anyone who visits.

Geography and climate of Seychelles

The Republic of Seychelles is an archipelago nation located in the Indian Ocean, east of mainland Africa. The country is made up of 115 islands, which are divided into two main groups: the Inner Islands and the Outer Islands. The Inner Islands are the larger and more developed of the two groups, and include the main islands of Mahe, Praslin, and La Digue. The Outer Islands are smaller and more remote, and are home to a number of smaller, uninhabited islands.

The geography of Seychelles is varied and diverse, with a mix of mountainous and low-lying terrain. The highest point in the country is the Morne Seychellois, which stands at 2,992 feet (913 meters). Seychelles has a number of beautiful beaches and lagoons, as well as forests, mountains, and wetlands.

The climate in Seychelles is tropical and humid, with temperatures ranging from around 77°F (25°C) in the winter to around 87°F (30°C) in the summer. The country has a rainy season from November to March, and a dry season from April to

October. Seychelles is known for its warm and sunny weather, with plenty of sunshine throughout the year.

History and Culture you'll find in Seychelles

Seychelles has a rich history that dates back to the 16th century, when it was first discovered by Portuguese explorers. The islands were later claimed by the French in 1756, and then by the British in 1814. Seychelles gained independence in 1976 and has been a sovereign nation ever since.

The culture of Seychelles is a blend of African, Asian, and European influences. The majority of the population is of African descent, with a small minority of Asian and European ancestry. The official languages of Seychelles are Creole, English, and French.

Seychelles is known for its diverse and colorful art, music, and dance. Traditional Creole music and dance styles such as the moutya and sega are popular on the islands. Seychelles also has a thriving culinary scene, with a mix of Creole, Indian, and Chinese influences.

Seychelles is home to a number of historic landmarks, including the Victoria Clock Tower, the National Museum, and the Takamaka Rum

Distillery. Seychelles is also home to a number of beautiful national parks and nature reserves, such as the Aldabra Atoll and the Vallée de Mai, where visitors can learn about the island's unique flora and fauna.

Aldabra Atoll

Transportation hacks in Seychelles

Here are few transportation hacks you'll be needing in your stay in Seychelles:

•Rent a car: Renting a car is a convenient and affordable way to explore Seychelles. There are a number of rental agencies on the islands, and prices start at around $30 per day.

•Use public buses: Seychelles has a network of public buses that serve the main islands of Mahe, Praslin, and La Digue. Buses are cheap and reliable, and tickets can be purchased on board.

•Take a taxi: Taxis are widely available on the islands, and can be a convenient way to get around. Prices are fixed by the government, and rates are posted in the taxi.

•Rent a scooter or bicycle: Renting a scooter or bicycle is a great way to explore the islands at your own pace. Scooter rentals start at around $20 per day, and bicycle rentals start at around $10 per day.

•Use ferries: Ferries operate between the main islands of Mahe, Praslin, and La Digue, and are a

cheap and convenient way to get around. Tickets can be purchased at the ferry terminal or online.
•Hire a private driver: If you prefer the convenience of having a private driver, there are a number of companies that offer private car and driver services on the islands. Prices start at around $80 per day.

Accommodation tips in Seychelles: List of Affordable hotels

•Choose the right location: Seychelles has a number of beautiful beaches and resorts, so be sure to choose a location that suits your interests and budget.

•Consider your budget: Accommodation prices in Seychelles vary widely, from luxury resorts to budget guesthouses. Decide on your budget before booking and be sure to shop around to find the best deal.

•Look for deals and discounts: There are often discounts and special offers available for accommodation in Seychelles, so be sure to keep an eye out for these.

•Book in advance: Seychelles is a popular destination, so be sure to book your accommodation in advance to avoid disappointment.

•Check the amenities: Be sure to check the amenities offered by your accommodation, such as a pool, restaurant, or fitness center.

•Read reviews: Before booking, be sure to read reviews from other travelers to get an idea of the quality of the accommodation and the level of service.

List of affordable hotels:

•B&B Guesthouse - Mahe Island - from $45 per night
•Chez Liza Guesthouse - Praslin Island - from $60 per night
•Casa D'Ange - La Digue Island - from $70 per night
•Le Jardin du Roi - Mahe Island - from $80 per night
•The Gecko Guesthouse - Praslin Island - from $90 per night
•Coco de Mer Hotel - Praslin Island - from $100 per night
•Chez Mari Guesthouse - Mahe Island - from $110 per night
•Happy Journey Guesthouse - La Digue Island - from $120 per night
•The Old Market Guesthouse - Mahe Island - from $130 per night
•La Digue Island Lodge - La Digue Island - from $140 per night

What to wear in Seychelles

Seychelles has a tropical climate, with high temperatures and high humidity throughout the year. It is recommended to dress in lightweight, breathable clothing that will keep you cool and comfortable. Here are some tips on what to wear in Seychelles:

•Light cotton or linen shirts and pants: These materials are light and breathable, and will keep you cool in the hot and humid climate.
•Dresses and skirts: Dresses and skirts are a popular choice for women in Seychelles, as they are comfortable and easy to wear in the heat.
•Sunhat and sunglasses: A sunhat and sunglasses are essential to protect your head and eyes from the strong sun.
•Sandals or flip-flops: Sandals or flip-flops are a practical choice for footwear in Seychelles, as they are easy to wear and easy to pack.
•Swimsuit: Don't forget to pack a swimsuit, as the beaches and water activities are a major attraction in Seychelles.
•Light rain jacket: It is a good idea to pack a lightweight rain jacket in case of sudden rain showers, as they are common in Seychelles.

Delicious Foods and Drink you'll find in Seychelles

Seychelles is known for its diverse and flavorful cuisine, which combines African, Asian, and European influences. Here are some popular foods and drinks you'll find in Seychelles:

1. Curry: Curry is a popular dish in Seychelles, with a mix of Indian and African flavors. It is usually made with chicken, fish, or vegetables, and served with rice or roti.

2. Grilled seafood: Seychelles is surrounded by the Indian Ocean, so it's no surprise that seafood is a staple of the local cuisine. Grilled seafood such as tuna, swordfish, and octopus are popular dishes on the islands

3. Roti: Roti is a flatbread made with flour and water, and is a staple of Seychelles diet. It is often served with curry or other savory dishes.

4. Fresh fruit: Seychelles is home to a variety of tropical fruits, including bananas, mangoes, papayas, and pineapples. Fresh fruit is often served as a snack or dessert.

5. Takamaka rum: Seychelles is home to the
Takamaka Rum Distillery, which produces a variety
of rums using locally grown sugarcane. Takamaka
rum is a popular drink on the islands.

6. Coconut water: Coconut water is a popular drink in Seychelles, and is often served fresh and cold from a coconut. It is a refreshing and hydrating drink, perfect for the hot and humid climate.

Things to do when you spend time in Seychelles

•Visit the beaches: Seychelles is home to some of the most beautiful beaches in the world, with crystal clear waters and pristine white sands. Some popular beaches to visit include Anse Lazio on Praslin Island and Anse Source d'Argent on La Digue Island.

•Go snorkeling or diving: Seychelles has a rich marine life, with a variety of coral reefs, fish, and other marine animals. Snorkeling and diving are popular activities in Seychelles, and there are a number of dive centers on the islands.

•Visit the national parks: Seychelles is home to a number of beautiful national parks and nature reserves, including the Vallée de Mai on Praslin Island and the Aldabra Atoll. These parks are home to a variety of unique flora and fauna, and are great for nature lovers.

•Take a boat tour: Seychelles has a number of small islands and islets that are only accessible by boat. Taking a boat tour is a great way to explore the beauty of Seychelles and see some of the more remote parts of the islands.

•Go hiking: Seychelles has a number of beautiful trails and hiking routes, ranging from easy to challenging. Hiking is a great way to explore the beauty of the islands and see some of the more remote areas.

•Try the local cuisine: Seychelles has a diverse and flavorful cuisine, with a mix of African, Asian, and European influences. Be sure to try some of the local dishes and drinks while you're in Seychelles.

Health and Safety Tips

•Get vaccinated: It is recommended to get vaccinated against common diseases such as typhoid, hepatitis A and B, Covid-19 and yellow fever before traveling to Seychelles.

•Practice safe sex: HIV and other sexually transmitted infections are a concern in Seychelles, so it is important to practice safe sex and use condoms.

•Protect yourself from the sun: The sun in Seychelles is strong, and it is important to protect your skin from sunburn and skin cancer. Wear sunscreen with a high SPF, and avoid prolonged exposure to the sun.

•Drink bottled water: It is recommended to drink bottled water while in Seychelles, as the tap water may not be safe to drink.

•Be aware of your surroundings: Seychelles is generally a safe destination, but it is still important to be aware of your surroundings and take precautions to protect yourself and your belongings.

•Seek medical attention if needed: If you fall ill or get injured while in Seychelles, it is important to seek medical attention as soon as possible. Seychelles has good medical facilities, but it is

always a good idea to have travel insurance in case
of emergencies.

Tips and practical information

•Language: The official languages of Seychelles are Creole, English, and French. Most locals are fluent in English and French, and many also speak Creole.
•Currency: The currency in Seychelles is the Seychellois Rupee (SCR). Credit cards are widely accepted on the islands, but it is a good idea to have some cash on hand for small purchases and tips.
•Time zone: Seychelles is in the Eastern Africa Time Zone (EAT), which is three hours ahead of Coordinated Universal Time (UTC).
•Electricity: The electricity in Seychelles is 220-240 volts, with a frequency of 50 Hz. The outlets are of the three-pin type, so you may need an adapter if you are coming from a country with a different electrical system.
•Water: It is recommended to drink bottled water while in Seychelles, as the tap water may not be safe to drink.
•Tipping: Tipping is not expected in Seychelles, but it is appreciated in the service industry. A 10% tip is considered generous, but it is up to your discretion.

Here are some landmarks in Seychelles

Vallee de Mai Nature Reserve

Anse Source d'Argent Beach

Victoria Clocktower

The Seychelles National Museum

I hope that this travel guide has helped you plan your trip to the beautiful Seychelles and discover all that this stunning archipelago has to offer. From the breathtaking beaches to the rich culture and history, Seychelles has something for everyone. As you explore the islands, be sure to take time to appreciate the natural beauty and respect the local culture and environment. And don't forget to try some of the delicious local cuisine and sip on refreshing coconut water. Thank you for choosing this guide and we hope you have an unforgettable trip to Seychelles!"

"Seychelles is a destination like no other, with its stunning beaches, rich culture, and unique flora and fauna. We hope this guide has helped you plan your trip and discover all the amazing things Seychelles has to offer. Be sure to take advantage of the many activities and attractions on the islands, such as snorkeling and diving, hiking, and visiting the national parks. And don't forget to try some of the local dishes and drinks, such as curry and Takamaka rum. Safe travels and we hope you have an amazing trip to Seychelles!"

"As you conclude your trip to Seychelles, we hope that you have had an unforgettable experience and discovered all the amazing things this beautiful archipelago has to offer. From the crystal clear waters and white sandy beaches to the rich culture and history, Seychelles is a truly special place. We hope this guide has been helpful in planning your trip and experiencing all Seychelles has to offer. Thank you for choosing this guide and we hope you have a safe and enjoyable trip."